Prai

FIAT LUX

Fiat Lux by Paula Abramo is a great story about the human journey and courage, marvelously captured in the poetics of everyday life.

— **Lucia Duero**, *Words Without Borders*

There are those who think that in the beginning came light and the transparent word. In *Fiat Lux*—a book as dazzling as a match at the moment of ignition—Paula Abramo shows that in the beginning came translation and exile, friction and chiaroscuro. And she does this with a musicality, verbal imagination, educated humor and historical and political consciousness rarely seen in her generation, or in any other.

— **Ezequiel Zaidenwerg**, author of *50 estados: 13 poetas* and *Lyric Poetry is Dead*

Paula Abramo renders enormities—exile, prison, geography, industrial chemistry—with sinuous precision. Here is a powerful sense of lives lived at the behest of various forces—economic, political, corporate—yet free in the deep, explicit sense of a hand striking a match. The sheer dynamism of this collection casts a steady, inventive spell.

— **Baron Wormser**, author of *Scattered Chapters: New and Selected Poems* and *Legends of the Slow Explosion*

The writing in *Fiat Lux* confirms the good news: the opening of new channels in Mexican poetry after years of stagnation.

— *La Tempestad*, Mexico City

One of the best collections by young authors in recent years, highly polished poetry that takes up the most concrete things without ever becoming prosaic, that joins classical references with the most contemporary poetics while effortlessly displaying an enormous range of expressive resources.

— **Elsa Cross**, author of *Jaguar, Espirales* and winner of Mexico's Xavier Villurrutia Prize

Fiat Lux is poetry of high quality in its minute attention to detail, its exploration of the possibility of language, and an original poetic voice that explores lyricism without relying on 'elevated' conventions of diction or tone.

— **Paulo da Luz Moreira**, *Caracol*, University of São Paulo.

Paula Abramo's *Fiat Lux*—a mesmerizing exploration of the borders between languages, countries, generations, and histories both epic and intimate in scope—is among the most remarkable works in contemporary Mexican poetry. And Dick Cluster's English translation of these rich and intricate poems makes me want to stand up and cheer: it crackles, glimmers, sings. Together, poet and translator bring us a breathtaking polyphony, a thousand lit matches, a radiance that changes and grows with every read.

— **Robin Myers**, poet & translator, author of *Having/Tener* and *Else/Lo demás*, translator of Cristina Rivera Garza and Andrés Neuman

By illuminating, like the match's flame, the instant's contour in the fog of time, this subtle book—the best poetry book I've read in many years—reveals more than what it suggests and suggests more than what it reveals.

— **Pedro Poitevin**, Salem State University, author of *Perplejidades*

After reading this amazing, unique and mind-blowing little book, readers will think differently about words like pain or identity or family. Paula Abramo proves that there are territories where only poetry can take us.

— **Alejandro Zambra**, author of *Chilean Poet* and *Multiple Choice*

FIAT LUX

FLOWERSONG
PRESS

by
PAULA ABRAMO

Translated by
DICK CLUSTER

FLOWERSONG
PRESS

FlowerSong Press
Copyright © 2022 by Paula Abramo
Translation copyright ©2022 by Dick Cluster
ISBN: 978-1-953447-44-9
Library of Congress Control Number: 9781953447449

Published by FlowerSong Press
in the United States of America.
www.flowersongpress.com

Translated by Dick Cluster
Cover Design by Edward Vidaurre
Set in Adobe Garamond Pro

NOTICE: SCHOOLS AND BUSINESSES
FlowerSong Press offers copies of this book at quantity discount with bulk
purchase for educational, business, or sales promotional use. For information,
please email the Publisher at info@flowersongpress.com.

Acknowledgements

Fiat Lux was first published by Fondo Editorial Tierra Adentro (Mexico City, 2012) and then in a revised edition by audisea (Buenos Aires, 2020). The Spanish text in this volume follows the audisea edition with a few additional revisions by the author.

Versions of the translations have previously appeared in:

Another Chicago Magazine: "Fulvio. On the road to Chiquitos, Bolivia, 1935"

Asymptote: "In the Maria Zélia political prison, 1935"

The Bitter Oleander: "Class line (errant)"

Brooklyn Rail InTranslation: "Introduction of the anarchist baker Bortolo Scarmagnan," "Requiem for the *embaúbas*, "In memory of Anna Stefania Lauff, match factory girl," "Bucolic interlude," "*Hic incipit vita nova*. Maria Zélia political prison, 1935"

Hayden's Ferry Review: "Angelina" (2)

Lunch Ticket: "*Batalha da Praça da Sé*, 1934," "Letter to the censor, 1939"

Salamander: "Same river. Bolivian Chaco, 1945"

Southern Review: "Angelina" (1), "Bortolo plays cards"

Tupelo Quarterly: "Childbirth. Santa Cruz de la Sierra, 1941," "I'm here to fight epizootics"

This book would not exist without those who told me the most beautiful parts of this story: Alcione, Bia, Helena, Lais, Marcelo, Silvana, and Zilah Abramo; Alexandre Linares, Dainis Karepovs, Marcela Tostado, and Renata Montanari.

Parts of this book closely follow the letters written by Fulvio Abramo during the 1930s and '40s.

Other parts are recreations of a history that I did not live myself. My apologies for the many imprecisions in these.

Contents

Translator's Introduction

The poems in this book evoke the poet's ancestors who were political refugees from Italy and Eastern Europe to Brazil in the early twentieth century, from Brazil to Bolivia in the 1930s, and then again from Brazil to Mexico in the 1960s. At the same time, I see the book as a meditation on the act of writing poetry and bringing historical characters to life. In each poem, these two axes cross in the image of striking a match. The poet's grandmother worked in a match factory in Brazil owned by a Swedish multinational company, making the popular brand called Fiat Lux— Latin for "let there be light"—as is depicted in the book's sixth poem, "In memory of Anna Stefania Lauff, match factory girl."

That poem introduced me to the book. When the author read it aloud at a gathering of translators in Canada, the poem startled and entranced me, so I asked her for a copy, and one thing led to another. Translating the whole book has been immensely gratifying. Translation is always the closest way of reading a poem, since it involves considering the functions of every word. Translating this book of poetry has also been somewhat like translating a novel, because many of the poems fill out suggestions about the characters that first appear in earlier ones. Situations repeat themselves in parallel, like the set of Venetian mirrors that concludes the poem "In the Maria Zélia Political Prison, 1935." Abramo was a classics major in college and is a translator by profession, so it's natural that the border-crossing and time-travel involved in telling the family history are evoked by the use of multiple languages, including bits of Portuguese, Latin, and Greek. Since English is farther from Romance language roots than Spanish is, I have helped English-speaking readers by translating some of these phrases while leaving others as they were, in italics, in the original languages.

The Bay Area Literary Translators' Working Group was immensely helpful in critiquing and brainstorming these translations during our regular gatherings whether in person or via videoconference. Fabiola Carratalá—as reader, native Spanish speaker, and English professor—offered her takes on many mysteries and quandaries in email interchanges between Cuba and California that, during long periods of COVID-enforced isolation, kept us entertained.

— **Dick Cluster**
Oakland, CA

FIAT LUX

ANGELINA

prende un cerillo
            no me gusta esta falta esencial del pobre modo
préndelo
            como si uno a sí mismo nunca se imperara
            como si para imperarse fuera necesaria
            rutinaria y filosa la escisión
préndelo
            lo prendo y qué hago luego.

—Prende la estufa.
—Sí, señora.
Angelina es breve y requemada.
Las marcas de sol. No son de sol.
Sí son.
Son preludios del cáncer. Son herencia.
Sobre la hornilla, el aceite bulle en iras.
Esta cocina casi pasillo, casi tránsito a otro mundo mucho menos azul y más
    de orquídeas, de pereza, de flores más lentas que la tarde, humedades
    profundas, corruptoras, colibríes, *cruás* allá en lo alto, a contraluz.
Angelina va friendo camarones.
Guarda uno, come tres;
guarda uno, come tres.
Guarda uno.
            Come
                tres.
Angelina tiene el hambre de su abuela;
más allá:
tiene el hambre de la abuela
de su abuela.
Y un historial de retirarse y retirarse bajo el crepitar de décadas de sol,
sobre el fulgor insano de una tierra
más quebrada
que sus pechos.

2

No es la lengua, es el Nordeste el que le lame los dedos a Angelina:
la seca esparce sal sobre su presa.
Y son tan buenos estos camarones.
Los subterráneos del hambre lloran –sí, pero no siempre– *caldo de sopa.*
Lloran también esta charola
tan abundante y gris de camarones.
Lloran la madurada tersura de los libros.
Y lloran las rosas –cómo no– las rosas.
Y llorarán siempre hasta que el fuego.

ANGELINA

strike a match
> *but I dislike this essential flaw in the hapless imperative*

strike it
> *as if you could never command yourself*
> *as if that required, routinely, a sharp splitting in two*

strike it
okay I've struck it —now what?

"Light the stove."
"Yes ma'am."
Angelina is short and scorched.
Marks from the sun. No they aren't.
Yes they are.
They're harbingers of cancer. They're hereditary.
On the stove top, oil bubbles angrily.
This kitchen, more of a hallway really, a passage to another world much
    less blue, more redolent of orchids, indolence, flowers slower than
    the afternoon, deep, rot-inducing damp, hummingbirds and *cruás*
    silhouetted up high.
Angelina is frying shrimp.
She saves one, eats three;
saves one, eats three.
Saves one.
       Eats
           three.
Angelina has her grandmother's hunger;
even more:
she has the hunger of her grandmother's
grandmother.
And decades of stepping back of stepping back from the sun
that crackles above a sickly glaring land
more wrinkled
than her breasts.
That's not Angelina's tongue licking at her fingers:

It's the Northeast, drought sprinkling salt on its prey.
But those shrimp are so good.
The hungry subterranean tears crying —but not always, Drummond de
  Andrade—*for broth.*
They also cry for this platter of shrimp,
so full and gray.
They cry for the well-worn smoothness of books.
They cry—why not?—for roses.
And they'll go on crying till the fire.

PRESENTACIÓN DEL PANADERO
ANARQUISTA BORTOLO SCARMAGNAN

prende el cerillo
ya lo enciendo

Ríspido, el cerillo enciende el horno.
El siglo está acabando; para el alba
faltan unas cinco horas más o menos.
No importa la hora, sólo importa
el gélido rodar del cielo
por los ríos. Hoy es algún lugar del Véneto,
y el horno.
Y sólo importa hoy la bóveda del horno.
La harina se hace pan, el pan es carne.
El pan son estos muslos que despiertan
muy noche adentro, al roce de otras piernas,
para luego salir antes que el día
a iluminar el horno y la madera.
Y en cuanto brota el sol, el pan no basta.
No brillan las constelaciones cernidas sobre el suelo
si todo está astillado de gendarmes
y es necesario huir sobre un vapor.

INTRODUCTION OF THE ANARCHIST
BAKER BORTOLO SCARMAGNAN

strike the match
okay I'm striking it

Struck roughly, the match fires up the oven.
The century is almost over; just five hours left
give or take a few before dawn.
The hour doesn't matter, what matters
is the glacial rolling of the sky
down the rivers. And the oven, today,
somewhere in Veneto.
What matters today is the oven's vaulted dome.
Flour turns into bread, and bread is flesh.
Bread is these thighs waking up
in the middle of the night
brushed by another's legs
and then slipping away before daybreak
to fire up the oven and the wood.
But when the sun rises, the bread won't do.
The constellations, sifted over the ground, do not shine
when everything is shattered by gendarmes
and a steamship offers the only way out.

BORTOLO JUEGA A LAS CARTAS

prende un cerillo enuncia
la multiplicidad de su nombre en ésta
y otras lenguas cerillo fósforo
match misto *enunciando el chasquido*
fiammifero
lucifer
ardiendo en llamas
llevando la luz hacia el abismo
cayendo ángel bengala arrojada
pozo abajo pero con el fuego en las tripas
de su junco hueco
y no por tan diario objeto menos prometeico
indicando qué tan hondo
es el fondo
sin fondo
del barranco

Y he, pues, a Bortolo tragando
en las noches apenas sugeridas
por el vidriado retintín de vasos,
polcas, impúdicos *lundús,*
y mesas descuadradas bajo chismorreos y risas
y codos y cigarros.
Tragando.

¿Pero tragando qué?
Cachaça tal vez,
y sobre todo
tragando como vapor de amplio calado
las ranuras de su propio tiempo,
que aún olían a mantequilla
y a masa hecha migajas

tempraneras
de azúcar y de huevo.

Y, en consecuencia, el tiempo
se volvía azaroso, un enemigo
punteando en sangre y tizne
el abanico ingrato de los naipes.

Y así, una noche, el juego
      se llevó el sombrero y la leontina,
      y, otra,
      tres meses de bollos de melaza crepitante
para la sonrisa de la niña del señor doctor, y, otra,
el horno, y los rodillos,
y la anhelada gordura de una América
de café y polenta fácil con gorriones,
y de niños copiosos y rotundos,
que aliviaba los sueños
de ultramar,
y, otra,

—Llévese a mi hija, don Abramo.
Es flaca, pero tiene
ojos de lechuza,
ancas firmes.
Cámbiele el nombre.
Llévesela, don Vincenzo,
y hágala bien feliz
con sus comercios.

Pero entonces quebraron los comercios
poco tiempo después de la gran guerra,
y en el patio una camada de hijos
con gallinas cacareando, ropa vieja,
nombres de elevada rimbombancia clásica
que no llegaron a la secundaria, pero, en cambio,
le leían al viejo panadero, cuando ciego,
las obras de Kropotkin.

BORTOLO PLAYS CARDS

strike a match announce
the multiplicity of its name
in this and other tongues match loco-foco
cerillo, fiammifero, *give voice to the crackle*
misto
lucifer
bursting into flame
bringing light to the abyss
falling angel flare hurled
into the well but with fire in the belly
of its hollow reed
and though such a common object
no less Promethean
revealing the deepest depth
of the bottomless bottom
of the cliff

And so there's Bortolo drinking
away the nights barely suggested
by the clink of glass on glass,
the polkas, seductive *lundús*,
tables tipped over
amid gossip and laughter
elbows and cigarettes.
Drinking.

But drinking what?
Cachaça perhaps,
but most important,
drinking up
like that massive steamship
the fissures of his own time

which never lost the scent
of butter
freshly kneaded dough
early morning crumbs
of sugar and egg.

And, in consequence, time
turned hazardous, an enemy
marking in blood and soot
the thankless hands of cards.

So that, one night, the game
carried off his hat and watch chain
and, another,
three months of crispy molasses rolls
that brought smiles to the doctor's daughter
and, another night,
the oven, and the rolling pins,
and the dream of America
fat with easy coffee and polenta and hummingbirds,
and children, abundant and plump,
to ease the memories
from across the sea,
and, another,

"Take my daughter, Senhor Abramo.
She's skinny, but she has
owl eyes,
and firm hips.
Change her name.
Take her, Senhor Vincenzo,
and make her very happy
with your dry goods store."

But then the store went broke
just after the great war,
and in the yard a litter of children
among clucking hens, old clothes,
and high-sounding classical names.
Children who never finished school,

but, nevertheless,
when the old baker had gone blind,
read to him from Kropotkin's books.

RUDOLF JOSIP LAUFF, MAGIAR, APRESADO EN POLONIA POR EL EJÉRCITO ROJO Y GANADO AL BOLCHEVISMO

no pero la nube mira
qué gorda va la nube
pasa
pésala con tu mano y ya no pienses
si adentro magnesio ardiente
una esfera azul
rompiendo despacito algo muy duro te recorre
que estás toda de alambres en el centro
toda de uñas minúsculas copiosa
absurda mínima ridícula
encogida
y eres tan una migaja que la nube
—mejor mira la nube y piensa en ella

porque por el momento es obvio
patente confirmado una certeza
que una chispa
la llamita real y evanescente de un cerillo
no puedes
ni eres digna de encenderla

Pero si todo a cero
se redujera,
          si a cero el voltaje, si lo dicho
          por los cables
a cero
llegara,
si nada
          llevaran los trenes, y a cero
ascendieran los diarios, y a cero
las cajas de fósforos,

y nada engendraran
las costureras,
si callara el acero
de los engranes todos
en un instante,
y no crecieran los muros ni los techos
ni en humo en el buche de la industria
de golpe,
entonces, ya sin duda, entenderías.

        Eso te dijeron, Rudolf,
           o quizá no;

        hablaría
           el comisario del pueblo de la guerra,
          o tampoco,

pero seguro que te contemplaste los puños
florecidos de elocuentes sabañones
                  y no sentiste hambre
ese día,
lleno ya de días siguientes,
en que asumiste la guerra y el trayecto
y te vestiste de cuero,
todo negro.

Todo negro era el cuero,
y los vagones tantos,
y el peso tanto, y tantos los zapatos,
y el diario hecho en la ruta.
Cinco vueltas al mundo.
Cinco vueltas y media,
la distancia
rodada entre la nieve, el lodo, las tormentas
y todos, y tú, Rudolf, iban todos
hechos ya uno, febriles de estampida
ininterrupta,
camaradas blindados,
convirtiendo
la lama y el pavor
en himno y llama.

RUDOLF JOSIP LAUFF, MAGYAR, IMPRISONED IN POLAND BY THE RED ARMY AND WON OVER TO BOLSHEVISM

no but the cloud look
how big the cloud is
wandering by
weigh it in your hand and you won't think
about magnesium burning inside
a blue sphere
breaking slowly into pieces something very sharp runs through you
you're nothing but wires down the middle
nothing but tiny plentiful fingernails
absurd, minimal, ridiculous
faint-hearted
you're such a tiny crumb that the cloud
— better look at the cloud and think about it

because right now it's obvious
patent, confirmed, certain
that a spark
the royal evanescent flame of a match
you can't
you're not worthy
of lighting it

But if everything were reduced
to zero
      if the voltage dropped to zero,
      if the cables registered
zero,
if the trains
      carried nothing, and the papers
reported nothing,
and zero
boxes of matches
and zero the output
of the seamstresses,

15

if the steel cogs fell silent
in an instant
and no walls or roofs were raised
not even a puff of factory smoke
suddenly
then, beyond the shadow of a doubt,
you'd understand.

That's what they told you, Rudolf,
or maybe not;
maybe it was the people's commissar
of war who talked,
or maybe not,

but surely you looked at the fists
covered in eloquent welts
from the cold

and you didn't feel hunger
that day,
full of the days to come,
when you took up the war and the journey
and dressed in leather
leather all black.

Everyone in black leather,
on that endless train,
carrying so much weight,
making so many shoes
and a newspaper too
all enroute.
Five times around the world.
Five times and a half,
the distance
traveled through snow and muck and storms,
and all of you, you too Rudolf,
all of you went,
all made one, in a feverish unstoppable
stampede,
armored comrades
converting
slime and fear
into anthem and flame.

RÉQUIEM POR LAS EMBAÚBAS

permiso para hablar del hambre
ese fantoche
de mal gusto el hambre
ya no existe
dice el señor licenciado
y enciende un cigarro lento
que muere ocioso
junto a una silla rotatoria en que gravitan
>>> *cristales*
>>> *rutinas*
>>> *frutas de esmerilada constancia*
>>> *sobre una fuente azul*

para qué insistir en ese asunto viejo
si ya el naturalismo
y la revolución
las ratas, ya se sabe
ya se ha dicho
todo y bien y mucho
es demodé
mejor hablar del amor
mucho mejor

permiso para decir que acalambra
que como lepra el hambre
se extiende
en manifestaciones ambarinas
noche adentro
día adentro el hambre
polyeidés *tornasolada variadísima*

más allá de su espantosa cohorte
de vacas flacas
niños inflados

también hablar del hambre sin calambres
el hambre gris de tiempo
para pensar en el hambre
para decir
la palabra hambre
con su boca abierta
y después pensar:
de tiempo
de libros de
crustáceos de encendidos tintes
y de flores sí
también de flores
y de espacio para enunciar su colorido
desorden
de otra forma

Muchos miles de hormigas, miles de millones
negrean el tronco mirmecófilo, se arremolinan en los nudos,
pasean febriles por las hojas inmensas,
las pocas hojas inmensas, asteriscos superlativos,
de la *embaúba*. Densidad de la madera: 0.02.
Idónea para laminarse, rebanarse en finísimas astillas
paralelepípedas, y, en consecuencia,
ruedan sus troncos —nunca demasiado altos—,
ruedan
como si hubieran brotado para eso
y no para otra cosa.
Se empapa de lodo el poco musgo que los cubre,
y mutilados ya, muñones sólo, sin asteriscos, sin hormigas,
van a parar cilíndricos a los arroyos,
pues desde allí cualquier caudal los lleva al mar. Y van rodando
esta vez sobre las aguas, unos sobre otros, yuxtapuestos,
escamas de un reptil inmenso,
confundiendo con maderas más nobles y duros,
en la infusión orgánica del río Amazonas, sus perfumes.
Entonces llegan
a un punto donde hay hombres no necesariamente
musculosos, pero sí
relucientes, y grúas, y escalofríos de fiebre, como siempre.

Suben los troncos
al camión, suben
al barco, zarpan
y viajan hacia el sur
hasta llegar a Santos y otros puertos.

REQUIEM FOR THE EMBAÚBAS

permission to speak of hunger
that tasteless loudmouth
hunger is no more
says the lawyer, esquire,
as he lights a cigarette
that idly dies
alongside a swivel chair that twirls
> > *glassware*
> > *routines*
> > *fruits of polished perpetuity*
> > *in a blue bowl*

why harp on that old matter
now that naturalism
now that revolution
and rats it's well known
it's been said often enough
and well enough
hunger is démodé
better to speak of love
much better

permission to state that it brings cramps
that hunger spreads
like leprosy
in outbreaks of amber
in the middle of the night
in the middle of the day hunger
polyeidetic variegated iridescent

beyond its fearful retinue
of skeletal cows
and swollen children
permission to speak of hunger without cramps

the gray hunger of time
to think of hunger
to say
the word hunger
with its mouth open
and then think:
of time
of books of
crustaceans of brilliant hues
and yes of flowers
of flowers too
and of space to portray their colorful
disorder
in another way

Ants, thousands and thousands, billions,
blackening the myrmecophytic trunk,
piling into the knots, swarming along the gigantic leaves,
the sparse gigantic leaves, superlative asterisks
of the *embaúba*. Density of its wood: 0.02.
Ideal for laminating, for slicing
into the finest of shards, parallelipipeds,
and so they fall, these trunks,
they roll — never that tall —
and, therefore, roll
as if they had grown for this purpose
only for this.
The fine layer of moss around the trunks
is soaked with mud,
and now, without asterisks, without ants,
leaving mere stumps behind,
they roll, mutilated cylinders,
down to the creeks
where the next flood will sweep them toward the sea. And they go on rolling
water-borne, one atop the other, juxtaposed,
the scales of some giant reptile,
blending their perfumes with those of nobler hardwoods
in the organic soup of the Amazon.
Then they arrive

at a place of men not necessarily
muscular, but yes, shimmering,
and of cranes, and shivers of fever,
as there always are.
The trunks are loaded
onto the truck, loaded
onto the ship, set sail
and travel south
to Santos and other ports.

EN MEMORIA DE ANNA STEFANIA LAUFF, FOSFORERA

la palabra alegría *no dice*
salto al centro del charco sol abierto
no dice inmersión matutina en tu iris
flores de jacaranda arriba y abajo no dice
mira ahí está el mar no hunde los pies
en la arena cada tanto
no sabe al primer sorbo del café de cada día
                        la palabra dolor
                        tendría
                        que prohibirse
quien escribe dolor se obliga
a aclarar
dónde y cuándo y por qué y si irradia,
punza corta hiede o raspa por adentro o por afuera
o ambas
o si desemboca por ejemplo en unas ganas locas de
     romperse
todo contra un muro
o en discreta náusea
o en el absoluto pasmo del reptil que siente al gato
                        de lo contrario
                        es caligráfico desagüe de la culpa
                        fácil justificación del verso
en cambio
la palabra cerillo
algo tiene de breve y fricativa
dos o tres dedos que se unen la palabra
fósforo
algo dice de incendio pequeñito
pero ninguna de las dos explica verbi gratia *que:*

In principio creavit deus caelum
et terram.

Terra autem
erat
inanis.
Dixitque deus:
Produtos tradicionais da Companhia *Fiat Lux*
de fósforos de segurancía,
há mais de vinte anos fabricando
e distribuindo
fósforos
em todo
o Brasil.

Dixit quoque deus:
Por la niña, la mitad: salario del menor,
menor salario,
y en una de esas, si persevera
y paga
un cursito de dos años
se convierte en aprendiz de fosforera.
No cualquiera.

Dixit vero deus:
Marca Olho,
Pinheiro
e Beija-flor.
Refratários à umidade
do nosso clima
traicíoeiro.

Tum ait:
Además
no habla
portugués,
y el país del que viene
quién sabe
si existió alguna vez.

Dixit quoque:
Confie na mais alta
qualidade
da indústria sueca.

Atque dixit:
>¿Fosfonecrosis?
>Tonterías.
>Antimonio,
>clorato de potasio
>y alotropías
>rubicundas
>del elemento
>más fundamental.
>Su hija sólo va a moler
>un poco
>de cristal.

Ait etiam:
>Palitos de embaúba,
>vários portes.
>Caixinhas com belos
>desenhos
>colecionáveis.

Dixit vero:
>De ocho a seis.
>Que traiga su comida
>o dinero.

Dixitque deus:
>*Fiat Lux,*
>pensando sempre
>nas nossas meigas
>e faceiras
>donas de casa
>brasileiras.

IN MEMORY OF ANNA STEFANIA LAUFF, MATCH FACTORY GIRL

the word joy does not say
leap into the middle of the puddle in full sun
does not say morning dip in the iris of your eye
jacaranda flowers above and below does not say
look there's the sea
doesn't sink its feet
in the sand every so often
doesn't taste of the day's first sip of coffee,
> *the word pain*
> *ought to*
> *be banned*
whoever writes pain has to
clarify
where and when and why and whether it radiates
stabs cuts reeks or chafes inside or out
or both
whether it emerges for instance in a crazed impulse to smash
> *everything against the wall*
or in barely perceptible nausea
or in the paralysis of a reptile suddenly aware of a cat
> *otherwise what is it?*
> *a calligraphic discharge of guilt*
> *the easy justification of verse*
on the other hand
the word match
hints at something quick and fricative
two or three fingers clasped together the word
match
hints at a tiny fire
but neither explains verbi gratia *that:*

In principio creavit deus caelum
et terram.

26

And the earth
was
void.
For God said:
    Produtos tradicionais da Companhia Fiat Lux,
    safety matches,
    há mais de vinte anos fabricando
    and distributing
    matches
    throughout Brazil.

And God said:
    The girl gets half: a minor's pay,
    that's minor pay,
    and someday,
    if she buckles down,
    and springs for two years' instruction,
    she can become a matchmaker's apprentice.
    Not just anyone.

And said:
    The brands Olho,
    Pinheiro
    and Beija-flor.
    Proof against the humidity
    do nosso clima
    traiçoeiro.

And said:
    Besides
    she doesn't speak
    Portuguese
    and the country she comes from,
    who knows whether it ever existed
    at all?

And he said:
    Confie na mais alta
    qualidade
    of Swedish industry

And said:
> Phosphonecrosis?
> Nonsense.
> Antimony
> potassium chlorate
> crimson allotropy
> of the most fundamental
> element.
> Your daughter is going to
> grind a little glass,
> that's all.

And he said:
> Little sticks of embaúba wood,
> in several sizes.
> Little boxes
> in several attractive
> collectible designs.

And said:
> From eight to six
> and bring her own food
> or money.

And God said:
> *Fiat Lux*
> Let there be light
> always thinking
> of our sweet
> and coquettish
> donas de casa
> brasileiras.

INTERLUDIO BUCÓLICO

y no siempre son las mismas las circunstancias
que rodean la breve vida del fósforo
son variopintos los dedos
que lo encienden las manos
a veces siniestras a veces
mutiladas
o cubiertas de esencias
con un esquema de callos
siempre único
denunciando el oficio
con una mugre
irrepetible ¿tinta? ¿tierra? ¿grasa? ¿sangre?
con firmeza o amaneramiento o descuido
los dedos
—pero siempre con cierta prisa—
que encienden el fósforo
para hacer suceder cosas

Hay ciertas historias que sólo en los bosques mesófilos,
o lo que a éstos equivale
más al sur, donde las sierras
son colinas que poco pueden
de tan curvas, cuasimaternas,
con su forro oscuro de cafetales.
Allí, la cena se hace
de batracios
capturados de noche,
turbamulta de patas y cebollas
desmembradas en un caldo.
Como frutos del charco,
verrugosos.

Ciertas bondades tiene el trópico. Éstas

de descendientes de inmigrantes húngaros
que cazan ranas
para una sopa
con leche de coco,
en un pueblo de nombre inverosímil
—Solemar—,
de dislocadas torres
de iglesia
piramidales, resabios
de Budapest, de Lugoj,
de pueblos vistos por las rendijas
de un tren blindado,
en una costa antipódica,
donde las charlas
del porche, en rumano,
conspiran en húngaro, cocinan
en alemán, meditan, tejen
recuerdos de nieve en la tarde
de mosquitos
entre taza y taza de café con piloncillo
y jugo helado de caña,
jaca, mango, *cajú*
con hierbabuena
al caer la tarde.

BUCOLIC INTERLUDE

it's not that they're always the same
the circumstances
surrounding the brief lifespan of the match
the fingers that strike it come in many forms
left-handed, sinister,
mutilated
sheathed in scent
calloused in a pattern
that's always unique
that announces an occupation
through a particular distinctive
grime
ink? soil? grease? blood?
—but always more or less in a hurry
fingers firm, careless, or affected
as they strike the match
to make things happen

Certain stories unfold only in cloud forests
or places like them
farther to the south, where the sierras
don't amount to much, just hills,
undulating, quasi-maternal,
darkly lined with coffee trees.
There, dinner is made
out of amphibians
caught during the night
a dismembered mass of legs and onions
floating in broth.
Like warty fruits
harvested from puddles.

The tropics have certain charms. Like

the offspring of Hungarian immigrants
who hunt frogs
for soup
made with coconut milk
in a town with an unlikely name
—Solemar—
where pyramid
church towers
taste of Budapest, of Lugoj,
of places glimpsed through the slits
of an armored train,
a town on a coast in the antipodes,
where they chat
on the porch-front
in Romanian,
conspire in Hungarian, cook
in German, ponder, weave
memories of snow
in the mosquito afternoon
amid cup after cup of coffee with brown sugar
and chilled juice of sugar cane,
jaca, manga, cashew fruit
flavored with spearmint
as evening falls.

BATALHA DA PRAÇA DA SÉ, 1934

prende un cerillo
pero ¿si el cerillo no enciende
lo que debe
no inaugura la pausa nocturna
de las velas o el atarantado
bullir en los sartenes?
¿qué es lo que debe
encender un cerillo
durante el rápido cumplimiento de su estrella
tan largamente esperado
desde antes de la penumbrosa caja
desde mucho antes del baño de cristales en la industria
desde antes
antes
del astillamiento?

Puedes decir, por ejemplo,
que es superflua la distinción
entre los diversos tipos de traslación ciceroniana
si se les compara con el hecho
más o menos aparentemente insólito
de que las servilletas de Anna Stefania, ese día
7 de octubre de 1934, bordeadas de austrohungárica labor
exitosamente trasplantada al trópico y tejida
en los breves intersticios de ocio que dejaba el oficio
de fosforera, que las servilletas, en fin,
no cubrieron con esmero peras, manzanas apocadas
o hipertróficos higos de cultura nipona, sino
pistolas varias,
de modelos cuyo registro omite
esta historia de vidas más o menos simples, sacadas
(las pistolas) de quién sabe dónde y quiénes.
Podrías decirlo, pero el polvo de Reforma te distrae.

Polvito de oro y liquidámbar, vas pensando, sin notar la monstruosa
—por muy manida— traslación que perpetras,
corriendo el riesgo de que te pase como a Tales,
pero vulgarmente, es decir, sin nada sublime en la cabeza y en lugar de pozo
el coche de enfrente, que frena a destiempo.
En cuyo caso, muy merecido lo tendrías.
Bienvenida la hipotética
interrupción de chichones, cristalitos sobre el pavimento
mezclados con el polvo "de oro"
para dejar de andar pensando chingaderas
que nada tienen que ver con la Patria.
Pero pongamos que tu cuerpo repela, viene un tanto horripilado
por lo anteriormente dicho
y arguye, en favor de las servilletas, que en los días que corren, digamos,
el azar democritiano, y el choque de átomos y eso, han perdido el énfasis de
        antaño.
Y ahora uno se concentra en otro tipo de causalidades,
aunque derivado de éstas,
pero más pintoresco y sabroso de narrarse.
Y de ahílas servilletas.
Podría decir también tu cuerpo: gracias,
señores del *Departamento de Ordem Política e Social*
por perseguir a mi padre,
meterlo en la celdita ésa con otros veinte,
interrogarlo los martes con las manos atadas al respaldo,
amedrentarlo para siempre con gritos de tortura y bocas de metralleta;
y gracias al *habeas corpus* por soltarlo y al *AI-5* por perseguirlo
de nuevo:
os debo mi existencia, diría tu cuerpo,
y algo de razón tendría, aunque
no toda causa debe agradecerse, mucho menos si de ella resulta
esta oscura servidora:
polvito de hojarasca entre las ruedas.
Pero honor a quien honor merece:
Anna Stefania
guarda las armas en su bolsa de mercado
y no va a la fábrica de fósforos sino que parte,
muy chiquitita aunque de 22,
al centro de São Paulo, donde otras gestas ya pasaron
y otras empiezan a esbozarse,

y reparte las armas
entre trabajadores del sindicato de bancarios,
del sindicato de gráficos de diario,
miembros de la antigua Oposición de Izquierda,
anarquistas recién desayunados,
y se pone al frente,
y dispara
contra una valla de cinco mil integralistas *kalói kai agathói.*
Cantan encarnado júbilo las armas
—véase cómo aquí
dos tipos de traslación conviven en pacífico concierto
aunque sea épico el asunto—.
Y no viene al caso evocar el consabido simbolismo de los tonos verdes,
porque verde era la ropa
del fascismo armado y verde quedó
el pavimento; de esperanzas nada.
Era puritita victoria antifascista en presente del indicativo
y fardas vacías dispersas por la calle.
Gallinas ya sin vestes huyendo en estampida: triunfo
militar del Frente Unido, aunque una baja:
guárdese memoria
del joven muerto Décio Pinto de Oliveira.
Y de Fulvio, y Rudolf, y Lelia, y Livio, y Anna, y Mario
Pedrosa y otros cientos
que allí estuvieron y lucharon y vencieron
a cinco millares de fascistas.
Y vivieron luego, y lo contaron
sin tanto abuso de las traslaciones.

BATALHA DA PRAÇA DA SÉ, 1934

strike a match
but what if the match doesn't
ignite the thing it should?
what if it doesn't usher in the nightly calm
of the candles or the effervescent
seething of the skillets?
what exactly should a match ignite
during the sudden fulfillment of its fate
so long awaited
since before the shadowy time in the box
long before the glass fragments in the factory
before
before the splintering now?

You could say, for instance,
that the distinctions among
various types of Ciceronian figures of speech
are superfluous
when compared to the fact,
more or less apparently unprecedented,
that on October 7, 1934, Anna Stefania's napkins,
embroidered with Austro-Hungarian care
successfully transplanted to the tropics and knitted
in the brief lapses of leisure allowed by her job
as a factory girl, that the napkins, to get to the point,
did not cover tangy pears or subdued apples
or hypertrophic figs of Nipponese origin, but
a collection of pistols,
of assorted models unrecorded
by this history of more or less simple lives, gathered
(the pistols) from who knows where and who knows whom.
You could say this, but the gritty dust rising from La Reforma distracts you.
Dust of gold and liquidambar, you're thinking, not noticing the monstrously

trite figure of speech,
risking the fate of Thales of Miletus,
but in such a humdrum way,
nothing sublime in your mind, and instead of a well
it's the car right in front of you, braking with a sudden screech.
In which case, you deserve what you get.
Welcome the hypothetical
interruption, the bumps on your head, the shards of glass on the street
mixed with that "golden" grit
that block any more wandering thoughts about inconsequential shit
having nothing to with the Nation.
But let's say your body just grumbles a bit,
finds itself mildly terrified by the above-mentioned,
and then argues, on behalf of the napkins,
that these days, shall we say,
the Democritean theories of chance, collisions of atoms, and all that
        are no longer fashionable.
Now we favor different notions of causality,
derived from those,
but more picturesque and tasty in the telling.
And, so, back to the napkins.
Your body could also say, thanks
officers of the *Departamento de Odem Política e Social*
for persecuting my father,
cramming him into a small cell with twenty others,
interrogating him on Tuesdays with his hands bound to the back of the chair,
instilling fear forever with screams of torture and mouths of submachine
        guns;
and thank you, habeas corpus, for getting him out of there,
and thank you, *AI-5,* for persecuting him all over again.
I owe you my existence — your body would say —
and it would have something of a point, though
not all causation deserves to be appreciated, especially if what it produces
is the obscure poet scribbling these words,
the dust of a leaf storm ground up by passing tires.
But all honor to her who deserves it:
Anna Stefania
hides the guns in her shopping bag
and doesn't go to the match factory but instead,
a slip of a girl at the age of 22,

37

heads for the central plaza of São Paulo,
where some things have already happened
and others are about to unfold.
She distributes the guns
to workers from the bank union,
the newspaper cartoonists' union,
members of the old Left Opposition,
anarchists fresh from breakfast,
and she puts herself right in front,
and fires
into a wall of five thousand Integralistas *kalói kai agathói.*
The guns sing a carmine joy incarnate
— note how, here, two figures of speech
live in peaceful coexistence
to narrate an epic event.
And it would be wrong to invoke any well-known symbolism of green hues,
because green was the color worn
by the fascists in arms swarming the plaza,
not at all the color of hope.
The result—and there's no denying this—
was an antifascist victory in the present indicative
the Integralistas scattering like frightened hens,
their green garb strewn on the streets,
a military victory for the United Front, although with one casualty:
let us remember
the dead youth Décio Pinto de Oliveria.
And Fulvio, and Rudolf, and Lelia, and Livio, and Anna, and Mario
Pedrosa and hundreds more
who were there and fought and won
against five thousand fascists.
And lived to tell the tale
without too much damage from figures of speech.

PRESIDIO POLÍTICO MARIA ZÉLIA, 1935

un erebo bajo otro erebo
bajo un
tercer erebo
que desemboca en un cuarto

la ciudad amanece punteada de gorriones

de gorrión a gorrión
repta la miopía
el último erebo
de la serie se ahonda en otro

imposible
prender un cerillo pero viene la sombra
de mi abuelo
envuelta en papel cebolla
y golpes oxidados
de escritura clandestina

direcciones falsas
nombres encubiertos en un género fingido
personajes de una gesta reducida a abreviaturas
viene Fulvio
a recordarme
"no mires hacia adentro"

no mirando hacia adentro
el abismo
se desintegra en trenes matutinos
color naranja vagones y vagones y vagones
llenos de tibieza
resabios de baño apresurado y secadora
organizado apretuje
solidario

que se desintegra a su vez
por las calles deshilachado en estaciones
se distribuye en oficinas talleres mecánicos
supermercados
con la ropa vieja
opacidad raída
sale
se distribuye
y enciende cerillos que encienden cigarros
que encienden
hornillas que encienden
el rápido desayuno a horas obscenas
que enciende el día
a su vez hecho de días
puesta en abismo de matices imprevistos

Observa la huella de la gota:
la forma ovoide de aspereza denunciando
en el papel ya viejo,
ya de más de ochenta años,
¿qué

       separaciones,
       lluvias,
       goteras,
qué circunstancias aquí colegidas
determinan
la transgresión de ese cierre autoritario:

     "quema esta carta,
     no la guardes,
     no escondas papeles,
     borra, anula:
     fiat lux"?

En cuyo caso el *fiat* habría sido
un no quedar rastro.
Un destello sin opciones,
un no, más que un inicio.

Y mientras, graznan

los cerrojos
la única palabra que conocen: quién.
Y la pregunta encierra
la posibilidad del rancho,
la permisión del sol, el lapso
antes del golpe.
Quién, preguntan todos, y los complementos
circunstanciales y directos del pronombre
en su mucha variedad construyen
los barrotes,
los muros,
los días de la semana
interrogados:
quién te dijo, quién vino, a quién frecuentas,
quién te dio estos libros, de quién
son estas cartas
manuscritas.

Y hace años, de niño,
en sepia, lento, hundías el plumín filoso
y las planas
llenándose despacio y pulcras
para esto.

      Y ahora aquí, un diente podrido en la mazmorra,
      casi como una semilla que brotara,
      que echara una raíz cálida y gorda de pus
      hasta el pulmón.
      De quién son estas cartas de quién
      las recibiste.

Distíngase entonces el *fiat*
del *fiat.*
Uno es nacer de luz para anularlo todo: un cerillo
encendido al borde de una carta,
y que abre un hueco en el tiempo, un hueco invisible
en la retina,
como los libros de Alejandría en llamas, fuera
del campo visual, lejos
de la hipótesis de luz, y el otro
fiat que engendra

y expele
a sus contrarios,
lo negro, la guerra,
el suelo: un *fiat*
fértil, encarnado
en cosas,
no en ausencias.

> *Mamma*,
> los días
> son tranquilos.
> Traduje aquí un manual
> de elaborar zapatos,
> te lo mando con la venia
> del amabilísimo rector de este presidio
> para tu sustento
> y el de mis hermanos.
> Gracias por los trajes
> y el pastel de nueces.
> Felicita a la prima
> que se casa.

Calcúlese entonces qué complementos,
la importancia de qué completivas,
qué acusativos, dativos, determinan
la distancia entre un *fiat* y otro *fiat*.

Por ejemplo, esta carta:
prisa previa a la fuga,
gotas
que se acusan restos
de películas lagrimales
microscópicamente reventadas,
como globos torpes,
grávidos, precipitados
sobre la instrucción precisa:

> quema
> tu manía de atesorar papeles.

Pero en la celda, meses antes,

la luz entrando como una ironía del trópico,
algunos loros dibujados en el cielo,
en el horizonte
sonoro de la cuadra del presidio;
la antorcha
iluminando
el calabozo negro de Castell Sant'Angelo,
y los interminables soliloquios
de Cellini
con dios mismo,
ahora aquí vertiéndose a otra lengua,
en otro calabozo
—¿eco de aquél?—,
como en un juego de espejos
venecianos.

IN THE MARIA ZÉLIA POLITICAL PRISON, 1935

one purgatory beneath another purgatory
beneath a third
that leads to a fourth

the city awakes dotted with sparrows

nearsighted crawl
from sparrow to sparrow
the last purgatory
of the series sinks into another

no way at all
to light a match, but here comes the shade
of my grandfather
wrapped in onionskin
and rusty keystrokes
of writing underground

phony addresses
names hidden by changes of gender
characters in heroic feats reduced
to abbreviations
here comes Fulvio
to remind me
"don't navel-gaze"

not navel-gazing
the series
disintegrates into morning trains
orange car after orange car
full of warmth
redolent of the quick shower and the hair-dryer
organized crush
of solidarity

that disintegrates too
into the streets, frays into stations
disperses into offices machine shops
supermarkets
with old clothes
threadbare
there it goes
disperses
and strikes matches that light cigarettes
that light
stove tops that heat
hurried breakfasts at obscene hours
that light the day
made too of other days
a mise-en-abyme of hues unforeseen

See the imprint of a drop of liquid:
a rough ovoid stain
on yellowed paper,
now more than eighty years old,
what

       separations,
       rainstorms,
       leaks
what circumstances gathered here,
determine
the violation of that closing command:

       "burn this letter,
       don't keep it
       don't hide papers
       erase, annul:
       fiat lux"?

And the *fiat*, in this case, would have meant
to leave no trace.
A gleam implying no choices
more a negation than a beginning.

Meanwhile, the door bolts

croak
the only word they know: who?
And that question locks away
any chance of a meal,
any access to the sun, any pause
before the blow.
Who, they ask, and in all their variety
the verbs and their objects
attached to that pronoun
construct
the bars
the walls
the days of the week
of interrogation:
who told you, who came to you, whom do you see regularly
who gave you these books, who penned
these handwritten
letters.

And years ago, as a child,
in sepia, slowly, you wielded a sharp pen
and the pages
filled slowly and neatly
in preparation.

     And now here, in the dungeon, one tooth rotten
     almost like a seed that sprouts
     that shoots out a warm, fat root of pus
     toward your lungs.
     Who wrote these letters, whom did you get
     them from.

So the *fiat*
is not the same
as the *fiat.*
One is born of light to wipe out everything, a match
struck next to the corner of a letter,
that opens a hole in time, an invisible hole
in the retina
like the books of Alexandria aflame, outside

the field of vision, far
from the hypothesis of light; and the other
fiat that engenders
       and expels
its opposites,
the dark, the war,
the soil: a *fiat*
fertile, embodied
in things,
not in absences.

     Mamma,
     the days
     are quiet
     here.
     I've translated a manual
     on making shoes,
     I'll send it with permission
     of the most friendly warden of this prison
     to sustain you
     and my brothers and sisters.
     Thank you for the suits
     and the nut tart.
     Congratulate my cousin
     on her marriage.

Calculate then what complements,
what conjunctions, what subordinate clauses,
what accusatives and datives determine
the distance between one *fiat* and the other.

This letter, for instance,
in the rush before flight,
the drops
self-confessed remnants
of the lipids of tears
microscopically burst
like clumsy bubbles,
heavy and full,
fallen
on the crystal-clear instruction:

burn
your obsession with saving up papers.

But in the cell, months before,
with light entering like a tropical irony,
a few parrots drawn on the sky,
on the resonant horizon
of the prison block;
the torch
illuminating
the dark dungeons of Castel Sant'Angelo
and the interminable soliloquies
of Cellini
to god himself,
now here poured into another tongue.
in another jail —
an echo of that other one
as in a set of
opposed
Venetian mirrors?

HIC INCIPIT VITA NOVA. PRESIDIO POLÍTICO
MARIA ZÉLIA, 1935

fiat
espejos frente a espejos
frente a espejos
y sólo por lo azul se ilumina lo intangido
un corredor
con cuernos curva
de pasillos largos
columnatas
baldosas
que a la larga
¿conforman un círculo?
¿una rueda monumental
de cosas repetidas?
¿en la que empero
breves diferencias
a todo efecto práctico importantes
podrían verse
si arrojar un cerillo allí fuera factible?
entre un episodio y el que sigue
colillas de cigarro
abrecartas
torcidos una máquina
de escribir sin teclas
un caballo miniatura
cajas de cerillos
pequeñas luces
de artificio
a la tenue luz del cerillo
que no viene
¿indicarían avance o retroceso?

Manchas en el papel del libro:
mapas de la humilde expansión del moho,

puntual y lenta
en los armarios,
signos ya callados del trayecto
de dos o tres termitas
junto al nombre
Blasio Demétrio,
traductor de Dante
en el presidio,
y junto al nombre
Marcelo du Nancy,
agrónomo en Bolivia,
y junto a otros
nombres abreviados e iniciales
al calce de cartas
de caligrafía disímil.

Y, mientras, en el interrogatorio,
la multiplicidad surgiendo como única
respuesta a preguntas que piden
univocidad, asideros en el error,
indicaciones transitivas
que no vienen.
Importante notar aquí:
no vienen.
Porque para huir, para escaparse como
        agua
        baba
        sangre
        orina
entre los dedos del momento,
la voz se multiplica, el nombre,
la vida, y sus relatos y sus letras
proliferan mentidos
para apuntar solamente
al joven Fulvio, que lo asume todo:
cartas de conspiración ajenas,
nombres, firmas,
y así los otros huyen:
gotas de agua
entre los dedos.

Hic incipit vita nova.

HIC INCIPIT VITA NOVA. MARIA ZÉLIA
POLITICAL PRISON, 1935

fiat
mirrors facing mirrors
facing mirrors
and only through the blue is the intangible illuminated
a pathway that slides
at a slant
through long corridors
colonnades
floor tiles
that finally
circles back?
a giant wheel
of repeated things?
in which, nonetheless,
minor differences
important for practical effects
could be seen
if it were possible to toss, there, a match?
between one episode and the next
cigarette butts
twisted letter openers
a typewriter
missing its keys
a miniature horse
boxes of matches
tiny reflections
of the faint light of the match
that isn't there —
would they indicate advance or retreat?

Stains on the pages of the book;
maps of minor flowerings of mold
gradual and slow

inside the cupboards
silent signs of the passage
of two or three termites
next to the name
Blasio Demetrio,
translator of Dante
in the prison,
and next to the name
Marcelo du Nancy,
agronomist in Bolivia,
and next to other names,
abbreviated, or just initials
at the bottom of letters
written in different hands.

And meanwhile, in the interrogation room
multiple identities spring up as the answer
to questions that demand
his solitary answer, handholds amid error,
transitive attributions
that never arise.
Important to underline
they never arise.
Because to flee, to escape like
      water
      drool
      blood
      piss
through the fingers of the moment,
the voice multiplies its name,
its life, stories and letters
proliferate as lies
all pointing only
to young Fulvio, who makes himself author:
conspiratorial letters of others,
names, signatures,
and so the others flee:
drops of water
between the fingers.

Hic incipit vita nova.

FULVIO. CAMINO DE CHIQUITOS, BOLIVIA, 1935

y dicen las fuentes:
"instrumento fungible"
dicen:
"se requiere superficie rugosa"
señalan
dos tipos de fósforos
ya sea integrales o seguros
según el grado en que deflagren
su propio cuerpo enjuto
y condenado

la clasificación no expresa pero implica
silenciosamente
los rudos efectos del fósforo
sobre el sistema óseo del trabajador
sobre el sistema
decimal de las cajas
de la empresa
los pequeños accidentes de ignición
en los bolsillos
frotados por otro cuerpo
¿un cuerpo humano?
¿la barra del bar?
¿un balcón? ¿un llavero?
¿un puente?

pero faltan siempre
categorías
que expresen la florida gama de sus usos
las cosas que se encienden
que con los fósforos terminan
o principian

o sus modos de fallar
de absorber un poco el trópico
e hincharse avaros
de su propia semillita de fuego
en el pantano

Era, decía, paso tras paso un lodazal, decía, de cuatro
cientos kilómetros, o más, con todo y tmesis.
Decía que proninfas, que en la superficie del pantano,
nubes de proninfas salían de los capullos
y los tres compañeros tuberculosos en el carro
de bueyes
atascado.
Difícil el fluir del discurso en donde no caben muchos
adjetivos más que *difícil,*
tuberculosos,
y acrecentar que todo era huida
en el Camino de Chiquitos, en el Chaco
de Bolivia, mientras
ninguna noticia de lo que atrás
dejaban.

Y, sin embargo, en la flora
del Chaco había,
no se sabe si por la poca carne seca
o por los bulbos de ingestión dudosa,
abundantes
reminiscencias de otra semántica.
Así, entre otras cosas, se contaban
entre recuerdos de lecturas y juguetes,
ánforas griegas que ramificaban en toboroche,
y el paraíso entero de Dante intruso en una pitahaya,
donde, imaginando mucho,
algunos círculos concéntricos
y flores, entre charcos,
como golpes.

Y eso por no decir los jejenes, los enjambres
de tábanos, los ríos
llenos de pirañas, tapires,
y esas lagartijas verdes,
de un brillo,
sólo visible en las auroras boreales, decía Fulvio,
que auroras así
nunca habría visto.

Pero era válido contar: maté dos, te hice una bolsa
mi Emilia de nombre fingido, mi
fosforera, pero el verde
murió pronto, aunque yo
te pienso siempre.

Y para distraer ampollas, y el gusano
alojado en el codo un mes entero,
entonces volverse transitivo,
verbalizar florituras
que aquí poco caben,
tintes para distraer a la *mamma*, a la hermana,
como de cromo, con ricos ornamentos,
del tiempo en que pedía, a los once,
un libro de Salgari, plumines y breteles
para el viaje.

Y así, por eso, Fulvio,
vuelto todo afuera,
transmitía después, rememorando,
instructivos para ver garzas, consejos
para observar su vuelo:
hermosas en pequeñas escuadrillas,
mejores si solas, las garzas,
mais lindas que a Isadora Duncan.

Eso al menos dicen los golpes
de la Mercedes Selecta
más de sesenta años después,
imbuidos de paradoxográfica misión y promesas
de más *mirabilia* en el futuro.

Y por evitar al censor, los golpes
no dicen exilio, dicen:
"vine a estas tierras a cazar con mis amigos".

FULVIO. ON THE ROAD TO CHIQUITOS, BOLIVIA, 1935

and the sources say
"perishable instrument"
they say:
"rough surface required"
they identify
two types of matches
strike-anywhere and safety
according to the degree to which they
ignite
their own body,
gaunt and doomed.

the classification does not say but it does silently
imply
the harsh effects of phosphorus
on the matchworkers' bones
and the healthy ones
on the company's cashbox
the small accidents of ignition
in pockets
that brush up against another body
whether that's a human one
or the counter
of a bar
or a porch railing
a key ring
a bridge

but there are never enough
categories
to express the broad spectrum of uses
of things that are ignited
things that come to an end
or a beginning
with the lighting
of the match
or the ways a match can fail
by absorbing a bit of the tropics
and swelling up
hoarding its small seed of fire
in the swamp

It was, he said, one step after another through a quagmire,
he said, of four hundred kilometers
or more, all told and with enjambment.
He said there were nymphs on the surface of the swamp,
clouds of nymphs emerging from their cocoons
and his three tubercular companions
in the oxcart
stuck in the mud.
Not much room for the flow of discourse
or adjectives beyond *difficult*
and *tubercular*,
augmented by the context that it was all about
flight, fleeing,
along the Camino de Chiquitos,
in the Bolivian Chaco, without
any news of what they left
behind.

And yet there were
in the flora of the Chaco
whether because of running out of dried meat
or because of the dubious roots they devoured
abundant
reminiscences of a different semantic.
So appear, among other things,
and between the memories of passages read and toys enjoyed,
Greek amphorae sprouting branches in the toboroches
and Dante's whole paradise embodied in a dragon fruit,
including, with a lot of imagination,
the concentric circles,
and flowers springing from the puddles
with the force of fists.

And that's not to speak of the gnats, the swarms
of horseflies, the rivers
teeming with piranhas, tapirs,
and those lizards
that gleamed with a green visible
only in the aurora borealis, Fulvio said,
though he had never seen
auroras like that.

But he could say truly: I killed two of them,
my Emilia of the alias, my
match factory girl,

to make you a purse,
but the green
died quickly, though I
think always of you.

And as a distraction from blisters, and from the worm
that took up residence in his elbow for a month,
why not go transitive,
into flowery phrases
that lead far from here,
flourishes to distract his *mamma,* his sister,
chromed adornments
like the day when he was eleven and asked
for a novel by Salgari, and pen nibs, and suspenders
for his trip.

And so, later, Fulvio
turned inside-out,
remembering,
would offer
instructions on how to observe herons, advice
on following their flight:
so lovely in their compact squadrons,
and better still if alone,
the herons,
mais lindas que a Isadora Duncan.

At least, that's what the keystrokes say
keystrokes on his Mercedes Selecta
more than sixty years later,
imbued with paradoxographical purpose
and promises
of more *mirabilia* in the future.

And to get past the censor, the keystrokes
do not mention "exile," but say
"I came into those lands to hunt with my friends."

CARTA AL CENSOR, 1939

hay una cantidad inmensa
de mínimas fronteras
cuyos nombres y mecanismos ignoramos
por ejemplo la del tiempo
específico de retardar la llama
de un cerillo bañando la madera
en fosfato de amonio
o las de la llama misma:
el cono frío la zona reductora
y la oxidante
o afuera el umbral de quietud
entre la orden y su ejecución
y el momento de quietud
aparente
del que decide
mientras decide
si obedece

Viene Fulvio y me dice,
por la espalda y de cerca
me sisea:
¿Ves el término *azul?*
Pues no lo uses.
Prohibición sobre la frontera,
sobre ese limen básico del vocablo
cuando abstracto:
umbral que, si se cruza,
es siempre en detrimento
de atisbos más acertados, porque
el pobre color azul, dice,
quedó mondo y lirondo asociado siempre
con el cielo, la pureza y otros espejismos,
de derecha, casi siempre,

cuando
sería más preciso decir
óxido de cobalto, ftalocianina, silicato de aluminio conjurados para,
por ejemplo,
algo parecido al cerúleo enredado en el carrete
de la máquina Mercedes Selecta
que corre
y vuelve a correr
y corre
en la década del treinta,
en Bolivia,
y que corre en azul para
no correr en negro, que es más caro,
claro,
sobre un papel de ala de mosca,
más barato y ligero y casi
tan mustio
como para filtrarse entre las grietas
de la censura.
Fulvio viene, se sienta a mi lado y va dictando:

    Estimado censor,
    bruto misérrimo,
    más bruto que el cuatrero que te arrea:
    deja ya de abrir mis cartas esperando
    que yo, tan *sponte propria*,
    me lance al pozo, porque la *spons,*
    querido mío, la llevo al paso.
    Si son mi estilo y aventuras lo que buscas,
    léetelo todo, y luego cierra bien,
    muy bien, los sobres,
    porque está claro que crees que así te ocultas.
    Y en efecto te ocultas,
    te cierras
    junto con el sobre,
    dentro del sobre,
    para siempre.
    Porque, de aquí a ochenta años,
    de tu paso por la historia
    de esta historia,

no quedarán sino un vestigio de agujeros
y la sombra de un gris oficinista
con delación a sueldo del *Estado Novo*.

Eso dice mi abuelo
en Santa Cruz de la Sierra,
con su carrete azul y sin acentos,
y bajo una crónica que anuncia las siguientes,
llenas de indígenas de inmensos arcos
y tocados
y jaguares,
firma Marcelo di Abiamo
du Nancy.

LETTER TO THE CENSOR, 1939

There are so very many
tiny borders
whose names and machinery we do not know
the exact length of time
for instance
to delay the flaming out
of a match by bathing the wood
in ammonium phosphate
or the borders inside the flame itself:
the cold cone the reduction zone
the oxidizing zone
or, outside, the threshold of stillness
separating an order from its execution
and the moment of stillness
or so it seems
when the one who must choose
chooses
whether or not to obey

Here comes Fulvio behind my back
close up,
hissing:
Do you see this word blue?
Well don't use it.
A prohibition about a border,
a limen, the abstracted quality
of a word:
a threshold whose crossing
always detracts
from truer glimpses, because
that long-suffering color, he says,
is down to skin and bones, always linked
with heaven, purity, and other mirages
almost always reactionary

when
it would be more accurate to say
cobalt-oxide, phthalocyanine, aluminum-silicate,
blended together to form
for instance
something like the cerulean ribbon in the spool
of his Mercedes Selecta
unwinding and winding
to and fro
in the 1930s,
in Bolivia,
blue not black
because black is more expensive,
obviously,
as he types away
on onionskin paper,
cheap and light and almost
shriveled enough
to slip through the cracks
of censorship.
Fulvio comes, sits next to me, and dictates:

>Dear censor
>mediocre beast,
>dumber than the horsethief holding your reins:
>stop opening my letters in the hope that I,
>*sponte propria,*
>will throw myself into a well, because the *spons,*
>old buddy, I'm taking it with me.
>If you want to know me, my writing, my adventures,
>then read all my mail, and then seal up
>the envelopes, very nicely,
>because obviously you think that will hide you away.
>And in effect it does,
>because you're sealed up
>along with the envelope,
>inside the envelope,
>forever.
>Because over the next eighty years
>your passage through history

through this history
will leave behind just a few traces of holes
and the shadow of a gray office dweller
a paid informant of the *Estado Novo*.

So says my grandfather
in Santa Cruz de la Sierra
in blue ink and with vowels lacking accent marks
beneath a chronicle that promises sequels
full of native people with huge bows and arrows
and headdresses
and jaguars
and he signs it Marcelo di Abiamo
du Nancy.

ALUMBRAMIENTO. SANTA CRUZ DE LA SIERRA, 1941

el cerillo
revela las distancias
entre las cosas
acusa oposiciones simetrías cuando todo
era negro
y luego
todo al negro
vuelve

pero en muchos semejantes mínimos destellos
cuántas
revelaciones caben
el cable sucio y quemado en un rincón el vestido
rojo
inmiscuyéndose con tazas platos
sobre la mesa en connubio extraño de tiempos
y dominios
o la hamaca en la selva los húmedos bultos
del garimpeiro o del talador
de embaúbas o las gallinas
adormecidas sobre el posadero
del patiecito de Vincenzo o

cuántos alumbramientos
que duran lo que la llama
transitiva
del cerillo

los cerillos alumbran
como los partos pero aquí
muchas vidas a un tiempo
conjugadas

cajita de fósforos estos escritos cajita
donde mi cuerpo se asienta
donde asentado
imagina su cuerpo
de fábulas

Alumbramiento, parto,
aquí mi abuela
alumbra: pare un niño
de cabeza grande,
leniniana, Anna Stefania,
capitana de un barco
que es éste,
de fuentes partidas.

Y allí está el barco haciendo aguas
y ella al frente,
capitana de un parto
que es el suyo,
ordena, anuda,
enarbola una bandera de sangre
en las troneras más negras,
revienta Anna Stefania
como si de cabos tensos se tratara,
para luego quedar
abierta, roja
como una granada
a la deriva, entre la hierba,
una vez saciada
el hambre de las aves.

CHILDBIRTH. SANTA CRUZ DE LA SIERRA, BOLIVIA, 1941

the match
shows the distances
between things
reveals oppositions symmetries when everything
was dark
and then
everything goes dark
again

but in all those tiny flashing gleams
how many
revelations fit
a wire, scorched and discarded, in a corner
a red dress
amid a jumble of cups plates
on the table in a weird marriage of places
and times
a hammock in the jungle the damp belongings
of the prospector the logger
who felled the embaúbas *the chickens*
sleeping on thatch stools
in Vincenzo's tiny yard

how many illuminations
that last just as long as the match's
transitive
flame

the matches bring it all to life
like a childbirth but here
many lives at a time
brought together

a box of matches these writings a box
where my body takes a seat
and sitting
imagines a body
of tales

Illumination and childbirth are the same thing
in my grandmother's adoptive tongue
she illuminates, *alumbra, da a luz.*
She gives birth to a boy
with Lenin's big head, Anna Stefania
ship's captain,
this ship
of broken waters.

Yes, there's the ship,
foundering, leaking,
with her at the helm
captain of a birth
this birth
she gives orders
ties knots
waves a bloody flag
from the darkest porthole,
Anna Stefania bursts
and it's like tightened cordage snapping
and then she's
open, red
like a pomegranate
adrift in the grass
once it has sated
the hunger of the birds.

"ESTOY AQUÍ PARA COMBATIR LAS EPIZOOTIAS"

o también se prohíben
y entonces los cerillos
entre los dedos de un niño
que achicharra hormigas
mutila
caracoles
estudiando la crispación inmediata
la retrotracción de antenas
ojos y mucosas
son pequeñas lecciones de la materia
y de sus crudelísimos
presupuestos

Esa oscuridad del nombre que infla
al ser que imaginas.
Piensa
qué clase de rarezas, qué bichos,
qué monstruos zancudhorrendos
serían las epizootias
que tanto combatía tu abuelo
bajo ese nombre híbrido:
Marcelo di Abiamo du Nancy,
ni francés, ni brasileño ni italiano,
disfrazado de extranjero, disfrazado
de extranjero, disfrazado de agrónomo
en Bolivia,
en la década del treinta.
Y eran batidas inmensas
eso de las epizootias orientales
viajes de meses por montes y lagunas,
penetrando un país de sal y plata
para salvar al ganado,
entre insectos,

y cuántos:
escarabajos
coprófagos, como cómicos
Sísifos hediondos,
solífugos más sueltos
que la idea de la fealdad,
chicharras escandalizando metálicas
el campo antes del verde.

El viaje medido por artrópodos horrendos:
nubes de moscas negras,
ciclos marcados por mariposas
nocturnas, mariposas
blancas, guerras
de hormigas,
marabunta de insectos migrando,
poniendo a salvo sus larvas mustias,
y lluvias
de hormigas reinas,
avispas carnívoras, arañas
amputadas con gusanos dentro, moscas
panteoneras y otras esmeraldas:
esperanzas traslúcidas,
eclipsándose en amplias nervaduras dulces,
luciérnagas
marcando
las noches de llovizna
y sus olores.

Y allá en la casa, Anna Stefania,
revestida de paciencias y madejas
estudia y borda en espera del marido.

¿Cómo
rodaría el tiempo viscoso
de la década del treinta?
Todo rodeado de *mirabilia*, en un país
de mucha mina
donde no había comida, y sin embargo
era posible, sin alardes,

mear argentinamente
en una rotunda
bacinica de plata
martillada,
escuchando el tintineo de la orina,
que iba pintando de *ater*
(*atra, atrum*),
sí, de opacidad de tizne,
su descenso,
y, al mismo tiempo,
el tintineo
de goteras hinchadas por el uso,
que iban a interrumpir,
en la cocina de muy poco pan,
en la salita de exiguo mobiliario y cuarteaduras,
la plática del día,
llena de ecos.

Quedando como registro de la tarde
un mantel de flores que son tachuelas
en un mapa.
Registros de un paseo
por los confines.

"I'M HERE TO FIGHT EPIZOOTICS"

or they can be forbidden
and then
between the fingers of a child
who roasts ants
mutilates
snails
studies the way they stiffen
instantly
retracting their antennae
eyes and mucous membranes
the matches are small lessons
on matter
and its cruelest
characteristics

That opacity of a name that enlarges
the person you imagine.
Think
of all the strange creatures, the vermin,
the longleggedgodawful monsters
that populate the plagues
your grandfather fought so fiercely
under that hybrid name:
Marcelo di Abiamo du Nancy,
neither French nor Brazilian nor Italian
disguised as a foreigner, disguised
as a foreigner, disguised
as an agronomist
in Bolivia,
in the thirties.
The immense dragnets
against epizootics from the east
journeys stretching from month to month

through mountain and lagoon,
into a land of salt and silver
to save the livestock,
amid all those insects
so many insects:
dung-eating
beetles, like comical
stinking Sysiphi
wind-scorpions more fluid
than the idea of ugliness
cicadas spreading their metallic din
over lands that had once been green.

The journey measured by horrifying arthropods
clouds of black flies,
cycles defined by nocturnal
butterflies, pure white
butterflies, wars
among the ants,
hordes of migrating insects,
carrying their withered larvae to safety,
and storms
of queen ants,
carnivorous wasps, amputated
spiders filled with worms, blowflies,
emerald green
translucent katydids
fading into broad sweet veins,
fireflies
delineating
the drizzly nights
and the smells.

While at home, Anna Stefania,
cloaked in skeins of yarn and patience
knits and studies while waiting for her man.

How
did that viscous time roll on,
that decade of the thirties?

Surrounded by *mirabilia* in a country
with so many mines
and so little food, and still,
it was possible,
without putting on airs,
to pee preciously
in a round
hammered
silver chamber pot,
listening to the tinkle of your urine
as it tinted its path with *ater*
(atra, atrum)
yes, opacity of soot,
as it flowed,
and, at the same time,
the tinkling
of leaks from swollen ceilings
in the spare kitchen
in the tiny parlor lacking in furniture,
flecked with fissures,
interrupting
the daily conversations
weighted with echoes.

And, like a record of the afternoon,
there's a floral tablecloth, the flowers
like thumbtacks
on a map.
records of a passage
out on the farthest edge.

(FALSA) LÍNEA DE CLASE

borrar muchas cosas porque son inadecuadas
decir:
son inadecuadas por lo tanto fuera
de esta caja de fósforos
cosas tamañas como:

Bordadas en un mantel:
inflorescencias de toboroche,
flores del Chaco
boliviano,
como golpes ya pálidos,
en sordina de estambres y puntadas.
No la abstracción de la flor, la corola neutra,
el tono rojo que se da por descontado; aquí,
la flor felpuda, el borde
fronterizo de lo concreto, como decir
toboroche, *embaúba*,
luz de manganeso ardiente,
semillas de cilantro metidas en la olla de la cena
sobre un mantel con flores.

Las flores del Chaco borda Anna Stefania,
que ahora se llama Emilia
y es enfermera.
Y poco a poco va haciendo un mantel
de acabada precisión botánica,
como una crónica de viaje.
Entre un caso y otro y otro de fiebre amarilla,
traduce en fibras de algodón
rizomas, sépalos, pistilos,
bulbos y estambres de precisos tonos.

Y todo ese conjunto va en correo,

hatijo de colores, de costura y flecos
sin un patrón muy claro
en una desprolija
narración de cloroplastos,
y bulbos, y raíces y puntadas,
a ornar la mesa de la suegra
de anchas ancas.

Pero no adorna fiestas
ni alborota, con su estridencia silvestre,
la base diaria de polenta y panes.
Y cuando llega Anna Stefania del exilio
le dicen al entrar: esto es un trapo
que saca lodo y mugre de la casa.
Límpiate aquí los pies,
sé bienvenida.

CLASS LINE (ERRANT)

to delete so many things for being inappropriate
to say:
they're inappropriate so leave them out
of this box of matches
big things like:

Embroidered on a tablecloth:
the flowering branch of a toboroche
the blossoms of the Chaco
in Bolivia,
fading like old blows
into the deafness of stamens and stitches.
Not the abstraction of the flower, not a neutral corolla,
the red color taken for granted; this
flower is lush,
plush,
nearly tangible, as if pronouncing
toboroche, *embaúba,*
flaming light of manganese
cilantro seeds tossed into the dinner pot
on a flowered tablecloth.

It's Anna Stefania embroidering these flowers of the Chaco
only now her name is Emilia
and she's a nurse.
And little by little she's making a tablecloth
in full botanical detail
like a traveler's sketchbook.
She goes into one house and another and another
houses of yellow fever,
she translates,
into cotton fibers,
the precise colors of

rhizomes, sepals, pistils,
bulbs and roots.

And all this goes into the mail
a canvas of colors, of hems and fringes,
no clear pattern
a disorderly narrative
of chloroplasts
and bulbs and roots and stitches
to decorate the table of her mother-in-law
with the wide hips.

But it does not serve as centerpiece
for any fiesta
nor disturb, with its stridency of wild flora,
the day's domestic serving of polenta and bread.
When Anna Stefania returns from exile
she's told at the door: here's a rag
for keeping out mud and dirt.
Clean your feet,
make yourself at home.

MISMO RÍO. CHACO BOLIVIANO, 1945

¿un cerillo también sirve para
arrojar luz sobre un asunto
determinado?
y ¿si la luz son dudas
si no viene en forma de respuestas?
¿y si la luz chiquita del cerillo
sólo tiene efecto por contraste
evidenciando
la inmensa oscuridad que lo rodea?

¿Qué quedaría atrás
al abandonar el nombre?
¿En qué punto del trayecto
Emilia volvió a ser Anna Stefania
mientras volvía
paso tras paso remontando
las veredas del Chaco,
con marido e hijo,
pisoteando hierbas
verdísimas
en una especie de masticación
pero del camino?

Imposible saber si era tiempo de secas y entonces
la sed también acompañaba el viaje
de transformación y regreso
a los viejos nombres a las viejas
extranjerías,
o si era tiempo de lluvias y entonces
los pies se hundían otra vez en el lodo
y la amenaza de larvas
dermatófagas y de proninfas
valía otra vez

en la superficie del pantano
revisitada.
No acusa estos detalles
la misiva
finamente caligrafiada en papel de arroz
en la década del setenta
y encaminada a México, donde el hijo,
sentado en un balcón de luz
y cactus,
leyó el relato del viaje
de sus padres, de su hermano,
el relato de un exilio que se acaba,
dentro de otro exilio,
ya leve, de plantas nuevas, de pan
recién horneado, con una elocuencia de trigo
y cielos sin nubes
ni lluvia.

Nada de eso acusa la carta ni
en su fino entramado de bolígrafo azul
hay suficiente luz sobre las intenciones
de la presencia del relato mismo, quizá
prenunciando fines y reencuentros,
quizá discurriendo apenas.

Pero en cambio dice
la fina pluma de Anna Stefania
que las chozas
eran muchas, pobres, el relato
aquí tiene menos *mirabilia*
que la falsa y vieja partida de caza.
Y en las chozas, habitual el espectáculo
de la ictericia, presentísimo
el vómito negro,
y mujeres muriendo por racimos,
rojas de epistaxis,
gingivorragia,
a pesar de ser ya mil novecientos
cuarenta y cinco
y de Max Theiler,

que allí no llegaban
sus inventos.
Y las mujeres muriendo por racimos
y la carta
como un cuadro, destacando algunos casos:
la embarazada que pedía comida
y había que darle algo, una lata
de sopa, las últimas aspirinas
para ablandar la muerte
tan certera como el viaje
reiniciado al día siguiente.
Y así cierra la carta y no dice:
vine a cazar a estas tierras;
dice:
quisimos volver por el mismo camino
para reconocerlo
y comprobarlo, pero un camino
nunca es el mismo camino.

SAME RIVER. BOLIVIAN CHACO, 1945

Does a match also serve
to shed light on a given
subject?
what if it casts doubt,
the light,
instead of offering answers?
what if the minimal light of the match
works only by contrast
to reveal
the immense darkness all around?

What's left behind
when you give up your name?
At what point in her progress
did Emilia become Anna Stefania again
on that return journey
step by step
along the paths of the Chaco,
with her husband and son,
treading on the greenest grass
chewing up
the route?

Was it dry season, in which case
thirst was also part of the journey
of change and return
to the old names the old
status of alien,
or was it rainy season and so
their feet sank into the mud again
and the threat of flesh-eating
larvae and nymphs
reared its head

on the surface of the swamp
they crossed again?
No way to know.
Not from the letter
its fine calligraphy, on rice paper,
written decades later
and sent to Mexico, where another son,
seated on a balcony full of light
and cactus
read the narrative of that journey
the one lived by his parents, his brother,
the narrative of the end of exile,
read in another exile,
an easier one, with new plants, bread
fresh from the oven, speaking eloquently of wheat
and skies without clouds
or rain.

The letter doesn't tell any of that nor
does its faint armature of blue ballpoint ink
throw enough light on intentions
on the nature of the story, though perhaps
predicts endings and reunions,
perhaps skips right over them.

But on the other hand Anna Stefania's
fine-tipped pen does tell
of so many huts,
so poor, and her account
has many fewer *mirabilia*
than the old false hunting affidavit.
And in the huts, the habitual spectacle
of jaundice, of black vomit,
ever-present,
of women dying in waves,
bloody with epistaxis,
gingivorrhagia,
despite the year being nineteen hundred
forty-five,
despite Max Theiler

whose innovations
never reached that far.
The women dying in waves
and the letter
like a painting highlighting particular cases:
the pregnant one who begged for food
so they had to give her something, a can
of soup, the last aspirin in the bottle
to soften her death
as certain as the journey
resumed the next day.
And so ends the letter, which doesn't say:
I came to these lands to hunt;
it says:
we wanted to return by the same road
so as to recognize it,
validate it, but a road
is never the same road twice.

(FALSA) FRONTERA

la palabra frontera *tampoco demarca*
sus propios lindes
ni indica cómo descifrarlos
si cromáticamente
si en materia de tiempo
o de textura
y queda abierta allí
como una fruta
como un eslabón roto
que propicia la fuga
de sentido
un fósforo puede
denotar un lindero
asegún lo que encienda
para fines iguales
un anafre una estufa
de gas
un horno
o una fogata

Supóngase una casa a las afueras,
una línea divisoria,
una calle mal asfaltada y, de un lado,
casas con firme, ventanas, castillos; del otro,
apenas láminas
y aleros confusos y parchados
de cartón goteando
sobre el lodo,
y de ambos lados, termitas
conejos, hierba
crecida,
gallinas
corroyendo las sobras, lo nimio,

humildemente,
como una especie de óxido vivo y compartido,
para luego acabar
en caldos tímidos
a ambos lados de la calle, pero en medio,
un accidente rojo, que viene subiendo
la ladera de mangos podridos
y moscas:

Gotículas, red esponjosa de júbilo,
olor a cosa nueva, casi áspera
de tan tersa, y viene rodando,
cucurbitácea carcajada,
desde las tierras rojas de Jundiaí
a punto de rajarse,
retumbando su interior líquido
en ecos:
el paladar haciendo ecos, las fosas
nasales
con ecos
de azúcar y lluvia y caña,
cuarenta kilos de fruta
en una sola sandía,
casi como un niño gordo
vuelto pulpa
y rodando
sobre el asfalto cuarteado
entre sonrisas y pasos
firmes de expertos
tozudos en sembrar
la fruta, que,
dando trompicones,
se estaciona.

Aquí ya no fruta sino ofrenda hinchadísima,
la sandía,
medio torpe y absurda en una casa
que no tiene heladeras,
donde todo es el sopor de enero.
Y entonces

un lado de la calle, el de las casas amplias
donde cada habitante tiene un cuarto,
le grita al otro lado,
de seres apiñados bajo láminas sucias,
las gallinas corriendo a medio día
a ambos lados de la calle, y aquella fruta
rajándose
sangrando como un grito de azúcares
de breve
duración,
que se mezcla con la tierra, con
los gritos de los niños que se acercan
o que lloran a caballo en la cadera de sus madres
otra vez preñadas.
Cuarenta kilos de fruta que aquí se parten
convivio repentino entre dos lados de una calle
en la que faltan heladeras y entonces la leche,
los dones repentinos, los bizcochos,
se reparten así,
sin mucho alarde.

BORDER (FALSE)

Nor does the word border declare
its own boundaries
or teach how to decipher them
whether chromatically
or in terms of time
or of texture
so it remains open
like a fruit
like a chain's broken link
inviting meaning
to escape
a match can
define a boundary
depending on what it ignites
toward a similar end
a hotplate a gas stove
an oven
or a wood fire

Imagine a house on the outskirts
a dividing line
a poorly paved street and, on one side,
houses with slab floors, concrete pillars, windows,
on the other
just sheet metal
and chaotic patched
cardboard eaves leaking
onto the mud,
and on both sides, termites,
rabbits, weeds
grown high,
chickens
eating away at the leftovers, trivialities,

humbly
like living collective rust
to later end up
in unassuming soups
on both sides of the street, but in the middle,
a red accident rises up
along the slope of rotten mangos
and flies:

Globules, spongy structure of joy
smell of something new, slightly rough,
skin taut, as it comes rolling,
that chuckling cucurbit
from the red dirt of Jundiaí,
on the point of cracking,
the liquid inside resounding
into echoes:
echoes on the palate, in nasal
passages
echoes
of rain and sugar cane,
forty kilos of fruit
in a single watermelon,
almost like a fat child
turned into pulp
and rolling
down the cracked, pitted asphalt
among smiles and the firm
footsteps of experts,
stubborn farmers,
the fruit
quakes to a halt.

Though it's no longer a fruit, more of a sacrificial offering,
swelled so big,
this clumsy, absurd
watermelon
amid houses with no refrigerators
just the suffocating January heat.
And then

one side of the street, the side with the big houses
with a room for each resident,
yells across to the other side,
souls crammed in under dirty corrugated roofs,
while midday chickens run up and down
both sides of the street, and the fruit
cracks open
bleeding
like sugar crying out
though not for long,
melting into the dirt, into
the shouts of the children who come running
or who cry lustily on the hips of their mothers
pregnant again.
Forty kilos of fruit split in half
sudden coexistence between the two sides of the street
which lack refrigerators, and so, milk
and unexpected gifts, and baked goods too
are shared around
like this
without much fuss.

MARCELO, 1968

son gozosas las formas
en que el círculo
se perpetúa
no la esfera platónica no
en su pulcritud inapelable
digamos mejor:
una naranja
o mejor mejor:
los discretos glóbulos
de su cáscara
donde casi en perlas el perfume espera
el momento propicio
de encabritar las llamas
o mejor aún: una canica
no comprada
esa canica que uno encuentra
encerrando un núcleo de sorpresa
por entre el lodo
ocultando
su linaje de pirata de escorpión o trébol
o de flama o de agüita o guacamaya
entre la lama
es gozosa la forma en que esa esfera se subvierte
a sí misma
en todas direcciones
y más gozoso el modo en que subvierte
lo que sobre ella se desliza
un pie por ejemplo despistado
otra canica
unos cascos
a galope

Bye, bye, Brasil,

meu pai fugiu
y no dijo *baby bye bye,*
porque
addio diría mejor
a los padres y abuelos,
al residuo tan sabroso de la harina de Bórtolo en la greña,
addio diría.

    [Fulvio, treinta años antes:]
    No mires hacia adentro.
    Pero
    mirarse los nudillos
    ¿es mirar hacia fuera o hacia adentro?
    Depende
    de tornasoladas condicionales, por ejemplo,
    si
    los nudillos reposan sobre la mesa de tablón maltrecho en torno a un té
        de coca, tras enrollar un cigarro por la tarde,
    o si
    se les mira sólo de reojo al teclear en la máquina con los sobrantes de
        carrete colorado
    o si
    mesan distraídamente el pelo del perro del vecino,

Meu pai fugiu
E como? No rabo do foguete?
Un cohete
es un crisantemo de vías posibles
a partir del cerillo que lo enciende,
mientras corre la mecha y se decide
la trayectoria: qué
pétalo
seguirá el cohete, anulando
el resto
de la hipotética corola.

    [Fulvio, treinta años antes:]
    o si
    se les mira al mediodía, cuando, resquebrajados,
    los nudillos,

abiertos por el frío seco, que reticula con sangre el camino entre los poros
y rebana la piel como un carrizo partido en dos,
manejan un tráiler y evocan
—guardadas las distancias—
la Cordillera de los Andes
que los circunda.
En este último caso, mirarse
los nudillos es una forma de ver hacia fuera
aunque mediada e interrumpida por hechos de dudosa asignación
entre el mundo interno y el externo: el frío,
por ejemplo. 18 bajo cero y, a veces, en Potosí, 26 o 27.

Sucede que ciertos crisantemos brotan
en las fiestas;
otros,
en la cubierta de barcos al borde del naufragio.
Pero éste,
el que mi padre siembra al fondo
de los rascacielos, sacando del fondo
de su bolsillo un fósforo
de la compañía Fiat Lux,
brota en la guerra.
Es, por lo tanto, crisantemo de vectores contrahechos:
los verticales
no tienen sentido ahora
que la alarma cunde, y ya nada
pueden las canicas ni los corchos,
los limones y naranjas
que el compañero asignado arrojó a destiempo
contra los cascos y sables
a galope.

    [Fulvio, 1968:]
    Intransitivo, empero, el gesto
    de mirarse los nudillos
    cuando éstos,
    apretando la mano de Anna Stefania
    que aprieta a su vez la bolsa de labores,
    esperan, en São Paulo
    –fingen que esperan–

un camión, precisamente en la esquina
del Largo General Osório,
ojos mal disfrazados de hábito y hastío,
mirando el ventanal
por donde pasa,
debe pasar,
la silueta del hijo interrogado
cada martes.
Y si no pasa, y si demora
el quebrarse de la sombra en los cristales,
cada segundo, cada cigarro
oxidando los alvéolos,
cada vuelta del ganchillo en el tejido
—los dedos alisando las puntadas—
es como la constatación
de lo imposible.

Bye, bye, Brasil,
Meu pai fugiu
e justamente no rabo do foguete.
El cohete que ahora corre
hacia adelante, hacia la fila
del cuerpo de caballería
y lo retrasa todo.
Nube de tinta de pulpo, humo, retirada.
Pólvora. Un caballo
rueda, se desalinea
el oxidado horizonte
de sables a degüello.
Tiempo ganado.
Fuga. Una tienda
de brassieres.
Joven, cabello largo,
talabartero,
fingiendo indiferente sesudez
en materia de copas
y encajes.
Pólvora todavía en la ropa,
y los dedos
recorriendo puntillas, resortes,

calzones
de todas tallas
como si pudieran defenderlo.
Y no pueden.

MARCELO, 1968

so pleasing the ways
the circle
repeats itself
not a Platonic sphere, no
unimpeachably clean lines
but rather let's say
an orange
or even better
the individual globules
of its rind
like pearls, almost, where the perfume awaits
the opportune moment
to burst into flame
or better yet a marble
not one from the store
but a marble you find
in the mud
with a hidden surprise
a lineage
pirate, scorpion, shamrock
or china, agate, cat's eye
inside the caked crust of soil
so pleasing the way that sphere subverts
itself
in all directions
and better still the way it subverts
whatever might slip on it:
an errant foot, for example,
or another marble
or galloping hooves

Bye bye Brasil,
meu pai fugiu

but when my father fled
he didn't say *bye bye baby,*
addio is what he would have said
to his parents and grandparents,
to the tasty residues of Bortolo's baking in the fibers of the mop,
addio, he would have said.

[Fulvio, thirty years before:]
Don't navel-gaze.
But what about
examining your knuckles?
Is that looking outward or inward?
It all depends
on, for instance, iridescent conditionals,
whether
those knuckles rest on a beat-up tabletop alongside a cup of coca tea,
    after rolling a cigar in the afternoon,
or whether
you catch just a sidelong glimpse of them while you type on what's left
    of a red ribbon
or whether
they're absently stroking the fur of the neighbor's dog.

Meu pai fugiu
And how did he flee?
In a rocket's tail?
A rocket is a can of worms,
a chrysanthemum of possible routes,
starting with the match that lights the fuse
the route determined while the black powder burns:
which petal
the rocket will follow, annulling
the rest
of the hypothetical corolla.

[Fulvio, thirty years before:]
or whether
if you see them at noontime,
those knuckles,
and observe how the dry cold has opened the skin,

slicing like a broken reed,
blood mapping a grid among the pores
and flowing over the skin
while the knuckles grip the steering wheel of a truck and evoke
— making allowances for size —
the Andean peaks
all around them.
In this last case, to look
at them is a way of looking outward
although mediated and interrupted by events difficult to assign
to either the internal or the external world; the cold
for instance. Zero degrees and, sometimes, in Potosí, 15 or 16 below.

The fact is, some chrysanthemums bloom
during parties;
others,
on the decks of ships about to become wrecks.
But this one,
the one my father is planting behind
the skyscrapers as he plucks a match
made by the company Fiat Lux
from behind his ear,
this one blooms in war.
Thus, it is a chrysanthemum of opposing vectors:
the vertical ones
are of no more use
now that the alarm has spread, and
the comrade assigned to employ marbles or corks,
lemons or oranges,
chooses the wrong moment to throw them
under the charging hooves
and the swords.

[Fulvio, 1968:]
Intransitive, nevertheless, the act
of looking at one's knuckles
when they
tighten on Anna Stefania's hand
as she tightens her hold on her sewing bag,
while, in São Paulo, they wait

—they pretend to wait—
for a bus, there on the corner
of Boulevard General Osório,
their gazes poorly disguised out of weariness and habit
searching the plate glass window
for the silhouette of a son
who will pass by
who should pass by
every Tuesday
on the way to interrogation.
And if he doesn't appear, if the darkening
of the shadow in the glass is delayed,
every second, every cigarette
eating away at the alveoli,
every turn of the crochet hook in the fabric
— fingers smoothing out the stitches —
is like a confirmation
of what must not occur.

Bye bye Brasil,
Meu pai fugiu
Yes, in a rocket's tail.
The rocket that now shoots
forward, toward the ranks
of the cavalry
and slows them down.
A cloud of squid ink, smoke, retreat.
Powder. A horse
turns, breaks
the rusty horizon
of swords and slaughter.
Respite.
Flight.
A store
selling brassieres.
Young, long haired,
a leatherworker
pretending to some scant knowledge
of questions of cups
and lace.

Powder still coating his clothes
and hands
as he fingers edgings, elastic,
panties
of all sizes,
as if they could defend him.
Which they can't.

ANGELINA

—prende un cerillo
—sí señora

Angelina es breve y es ficticia
(las marcas de sol sí son de sol)
y vino aquí a hacer el favor de su presencia
porque existe el hambre, ese fantoche de mal gusto,
y existe la cocina, existe la orden
de encender un fósforo
y hay una riqueza enorme y mal distribuida
de crustáceos en el mundo, y de libros y de tiempo
para leerlos.
Angelina va friendo camarones:
    guarda uno y come tres,
    porque la llama
    —los efectos de la llama—
    del cerillo
los hace suyos,
trabajan
para ella,
y en la frontera minúscula que media
entre la orden y el hecho de cumplirla,
caben los ciclos, las repeticiones,
las guerras, el juego de espejos
venecianos, donde gestas
y gestas
y exilios
y barrotes
sólo tienen sentido si trastornan
el fin de ese cerillo:
si segundos antes de encenderlo
se opta por el acato o el desacato
y la *lux* que *fit*,
aunque pequeña,
no es ya la luz de un fósforo.

ANGELINA

strike a match
sí, señora

Angelina is short and she is fictional
(the marks of the sun are indeed from the sun)
and she came here to offer the favor of her presence
because hunger exists, that tasteless loudmouth,
and so does that kitchen, and so does the order
to strike a match
and there are enormous and badly distributed riches
of crustaceans in the world, and of books and time
to read them.
Angelina is frying shrimp:
            saves one and eats three,
            because the flame
            — the effects of the flame—
            of that match
she will make her own,
so they work
for her,
and within the miniscule borderline
between an order and the fact of obeying it,
lie the cycles, the repetitions,
the wars, the set of Venetian
mirrors, where exploits
and exiles
and prison bars
make sense only if they disturb
the match's purpose:
if seconds before lighting it
one chooses between compliance and disobedience
and the *lux* that *fit,*
the light there is,
although small,
is no longer the light of a match.

AUTHOR BIOGRAPHY

PAULA ABRAMO was born in Mexico City in 1980. In 2012, she was the winner of the Premio de Poesía Joaquín Xirau Icaza for the best book of poems by a writer under forty. Abroad, her work has appeared in journals and anthologies of contemporary Mexican and worldwide poetry, both in the original Spanish and in translations to Portuguese, German, English, and French. She is also a prolific translator from Portuguese to Spanish, with more than fifty books to her credit, and is co-author of "*Yo soy la otra: las mujeres y la cultura en México*" (2017) and the art installation "*Ropa Sucia*" (2017), both exploring the causes of the invisibility of Mexican female writers and artists.

TRANSLATOR BIOGRAPHY

DICK CLUSTER is the author of a mystery novel series and of histories of U.S. political movements and the city of Havana. Over the past twenty-five years, he has been translating prose and poetry by authors from Cuba, Ecuador, Mexico, Spain, and elsewhere, as well as editing and translating the anthology *Kill the Ámpaya!: The Best Latin American Baseball Fiction.* He lives in Oakland, California, where he volunteers as an interpreter for refugees seeking asylum in the U.S.

9 781953 447449